WHO YOU ARE

WHO YOU ARE

PERSONALITY

AND ITS

DEVELOPMENT

**by Robert S. Feldman
and Joel A. Feinman**

A Venture Book
Franklin Watts
New York / Chicago / London / Toronto / Sydney

Library of Congress Cataloging-in-Publication Data

Feldman, Robert S. (Robert Stephen), 1947-
    Who you are : personality and its development / by Robert S.
Feldman and Joel A. Feinman.
        p.   cm. — (A Venture book)
    Includes bibliographical references and index.
    Summary: Examines the concepts of personality and identity,
particularly as they relate to teenagers.
    ISBN 0-531-12544-0
    1. Personality. 2. Personality development. [1. Personality.
2. Identity.] I. Title.
BF698.F365   1992
155.2—dc20   92-25494   CIP   AC

CONTENTS

WHO YOU ARE

INTRODUCTION

What Is Personality?

When Max walked into his high school English class on the first day of school, he saw twenty-three other kids who seemed pretty similar to one another. They were boys and girls about his age and size, and they all looked a little nervous about the start of the new school year.

As they began to talk among themselves before the start of class, Max found that they all had pretty much the same kind of questions about the class: Would it be interesting? What was the teacher, Ms. Hayward, like? Would there be a lot of homework?

Max found that his own nervousness about school decreased a little as he realized that the other kids shared his con-

cerns. *In fact, he began to think that the class was made up of kids who were a lot like himself. Why, he thought, they're all pretty much alike, and not much different from me.*

But that didn't get rid of all his worries. He still questioned if he was good enough to make it in high school. He wondered if he'd be able to do all the homework, and make new friends, and succeed in this new school. He didn't have a whole lot of confidence, and sometimes he wondered just what kind of person he was.

It was the last day of class, and Max walked into his English class for the final time and looked around the room. The year had gone by quickly.

As he watched the other kids, he thought for a moment back to his first day in class. How could he not have recognized how different his classmates were from one another?

Now he knew better. There was Sally, who was the smartest girl in the class and who never seemed to make a mistake. Then there was Hank, who acted like a jerk most of the time. And Bill, who would patiently go out of his way to help anybody in the class. Each of the twenty-three students in the class was an individual, with special qualities and traits.

At the same time, though, he also knew how many similarities his classmates shared. Although they all liked Ms. Hayward, they hated her homework assignments. More basically, they all seemed to like their families pretty well, and they shared many of the same hopes about doing well in the future.

And what about himself? Max felt that he had come a long way in getting to know who he was. The year had not been easy. A lot of change had taken place in his life. But he felt good about how things were going. He had started out in a new school, and he'd been successful. He felt self-confident and happy.

It had been a good year.

Like Max, most of us come to realize how different people are from one another. Although all human beings share basic qualities and traits, each person is special and different from everyone else.

The study of personality focuses on the uniqueness of people. It looks at the characteristics that make one person different from another. By studying personality, we can understand what special qualities each one has.

Personality also helps us to understand how consistent a person's behavior is. A person usually behaves in fairly uniform ways, no matter what the situation in which that person finds himself or herself. For example, a girl who has an outgoing personality usually acts outgoing with her classmates, with her friends, and with her family. Personality forms the basis of this consistent behavior.

PERSONALITY—WHAT IT ISN'T, AND WHAT IT IS

Most people have an idea about what personality is. But many people use the term in an imprecise way. For instance, you may have heard people say that someone has a "good personality." What they mean is that someone behaves in a way that makes them pleasant to be around.

There is nothing wrong with this meaning of the concept of personality. However, psychologists, experts who study personality, use a more formal definition:

> Personality *consists of the character-istics that (1) make us distinctive from other people and (2) are consistent over time.*

The cornerstones of personality, then, can be summed up in two words: distinctiveness and consistency.[1] To understand personality fully, we need to look at both of these aspects.

DISTINCTIVENESS. Each of us is a unique individual, with special abilities, traits, and feelings. Taken together, these characteristics form a pattern. This pattern is as distinctive for each individual as are his or her fingerprints.

To understand personality, we need to discover what makes up this special pattern of characteristics. We must look at the causes of personality and how it develops as we become older. We need to see what makes people different from one another.

For instance, we might try to understand the distinctive parts of the students' personalities in Max's class. To do this, we would look at each student as an individual, and try to find what makes him or her stand out from the others in the class.

In one student, the major feature of personality might be a good sense of humor. In another student, it might be generosity that makes her or him special. And for yet another, it might be the habit of getting into fights.

Usually, though, it is not just one single trait that makes a person unique. It is a special mix of qualities that make up a personality.

CONSISTENCY. The second key element to personality is consistency. To understand the keys to personality, we need to look at how consistent people are as they move from one situation to another.

We need to see how an especially friendly girl, for example, shows that friendliness in different situations. Is she equally friendly to her classmates in school and to the dentist? Does she behave in a friendly way when she is sick or when she gets up in the morning?

In order for us to say that friendliness is a key part of her personality, she has to act consistently friendly in different situations. Of course, she won't *always* be friendly. No one could be friendly all the time. But for friendliness to be a central part of her personality, she must be friendly most of the time.

In sum, a personality has two key elements: distinctiveness and consistency. It is distinctive because it is made up of the characteristics that distinguish us from other people. It is consistent, making us act in similar ways in different situations.

THE DEVELOPMENT OF PERSONALITY

We are not born with a particular kind of personality. Indeed, in many ways young babies are quite similar to one another. However, the older we get, the more different we become from others. In other words, we develop a particular kind of personality.

How does our personality develop? Much of the work done by experts in personality has been aimed at identifying personality development. The study of *personality development* focuses on the ways in which our personality changes as we get older.

There are many explanations of how personality develops. Some say that to understand personality, we need to focus on the kind of environment in which people grow up. For instance, a child raised in extreme poverty would be assumed to have a very different personality from one raised in a wealthy family. According to this kind of explanation, people's personalities are affected most by the kinds of things their parents and other caregivers do as they raise them. In this view, we need to look carefully at the environment in which people are raised to understand personality.

Other explanations of personality have a different point of view. They say that personality develops in a fairly automatic way. In this view, it doesn't matter as much what happens to people as they grow up. According to this theory, an individual's personality will pretty much unfold in the same way whether they are raised under difficult circumstances, with few economic advantages, or under more favorable situations, as with great wealth.

As we will discuss later in this book, we don't know for sure which of these explanations is best. It is likely that some parts of each explanation are correct. Some aspects of personality are affected by what we encounter in our environment as we grow up. But other parts of personality seem to develop almost automatically, regardless of the circumstances under which we are raised.

What we do know for sure is that personality changes all the time. You are not exactly the same person you were a year ago. And you will not be exactly the same kind of person a year from now.

However, there are some things about you that don't change very much. One of the biggest challenges in understanding personality, then, is this: distinguishing how we constantly grow and change from the ways in which we stay the same.

PART ONE

THE
SOURCE
OF
PERSONALITY

CHAPTER ONE

The Hidden Core of Personality: Freud and Psychoanalysis

Have you ever seen the television show "Cheers"? When it first began, the show had two main characters, Sam and Diane, who were very different from one another. Sam was a playboy, always talking about girls, and getting himself into some crazy situations. In contrast, Diane was more formal, serious, and much less adventurous than Sam.

On the surface, Sam and Diane seem to have very different personalities. However, one explanation of personality suggests that the differences may be just on the surface. According to *psychoanalytic* (sy-ko-an-a-lit-ik) *personality theory,* Sam and Diane may actually share the same kind of personality. This explanation proposes that Sam's and Diane's surface differences in behavior are produced by personality factors that may be identical.

Psychoanalytic explanations of personality suggest that much of personality is composed of hidden forces.[1] These hidden forces, which determine people's behavior, are found in the unconscious.

The *unconscious* is the part of personality of which a person is not aware. The unconscious contains unpleasant thoughts and memories of events that occurred throughout our lives. Because they are unpleasant, they would disrupt everyday living if we continually thought about them.

Suppose, for instance, a young boy witnesses a gory traffic accident in which someone's arm is cut off. Thinking about the accident probably would be very upsetting.

Psychoanalytic explanations of personality would say that one way of protecting ourselves from upsetting memories is to push the memories into the unconscious part of personality. Buried in the unconscious, those memories would no longer be upsetting.

Because we are not aware of the kind of memories that we have in the unconscious, the boy wouldn't have to think about them much during his everyday life. In fact, he might entirely forget about the accident—in the conscious part of personality. (The conscious part of personality is the portion of personality of which a person *is* aware.)

However, even though the memories of the accident are in the unconscious, the boy might still be affected by them. Psychoanalytic explanations of personality say that even if we don't *consciously* remember our past experiences, our behavior is still affected by them being in the unconscious part of our personality.

For instance, the boy's unconscious memories of the accident might make him unusually interested in automobiles. He might collect toy automobiles and learn the names of different makes and models of cars he sees on the road. Because the memory of the accident was buried deep in his unconscious, no one, not even the boy himself, would know the reason for his deep concern about cars.

SIGMUND FREUD
AND
PSYCHOANALYTIC THEORY

Psychoanalytic explanations of personality were first devised by Sigmund Freud.[2] Freud was a physician who lived in Vienna in the early 1900s.

Freud felt that the things that people were aware of—the ideas and memories in the conscious—were just a small part of personality. He felt that personality was similar to an iceberg. Like an iceberg, in which most of the ice lies beneath the surface of the water, most of personality is hidden in the unconscious.

Freud thought that in order to completely understand personality, it was necessary to expose what is in the unconscious. However, this is not easy. In Freud's view, the unconscious part of personality tries to disguise its contents in order to protect us from painful or upsetting memories.

If the unconscious tries to hide things, how can we learn what it contains? The answer, according to Freud, is to interpret clues that come from dreams, fantasies, and slips of the tongue. By playing personality detective, we can come to understand what lies beneath the surface of our personality. We can come to see what forces make us behave as we do.

Freud's explanation of personality says that there are actually three separate parts to personality: the id, the ego, and the superego. Each one plays a different role in determining people's behavior.

As you can see in Figure 1, the three parts can be shown in a diagram. It shows the significance of each part of personality by its size. It also shows that most of the personality is located in the unconscious.

It is important to know that these three parts are not real, physical structures. They are not actually located somewhere in the human body. Instead, the figure represents a model of how the three parts of personality fit together. Each part shows a different way in which personality operates. It is also important to remember that these three parts are based only on Freud's views. As we'll see later, many people don't agree with him.

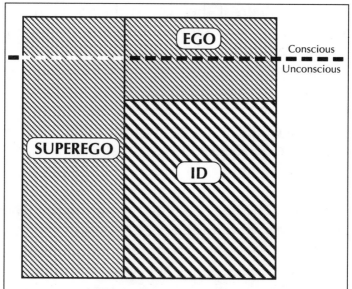

Figure 1. The three parts of personality, according to Freud, who believed that most of one's personality is hidden beneath the surface in what he called the "unconscious".

THE ID. The id is the most primitive part of personality. It represents the animal side of a person. The id's one purpose is to satisfy desires such as hunger, thirst, aggression, and sex.

The id pushes people to satisfy any need that might arise, as quickly as possible. It tries to reduce immediately any tension that might arise in people. The id also tries to obtain as much satisfaction as possible.

Think what the world would be like if the id were the only part of personality. People would be fighting over food. They would think nothing of attacking others if they got in their way. There would be no limits on what people would do to satisfy their needs.

In most cases, however, this doesn't happen. The id doesn't always get its way. We can't always eat when we are hungry, for instance. Because of the realities of life, Freud suggested that another part of the personality helps to restrain the id. He called it the ego.

THE EGO. The ego is the part of personality that acts as a barrier between the id's desires and the world's realities. The ego restrains the unthinking id. It tries to help people get along with others in society. It does this by keeping the id's desires under control.

In one way, the ego is like a company big shot with the job of maintaining order. The ego makes decisions, places controls on behavior, and orders logical thinking. Intelligence, reasoning, learning, and thoughtfulness are all found in the ego.

The ego permits us to lead healthy and safe lives. Without the ego, the id would lead us to try to satisfy our momentary impulses. We would never think of the future effects of such behavior.

THE SUPEREGO. The third part of personality is the superego. The superego translates the rights and wrongs of society. When you learn that it is wrong to steal or it is good to give to charity, the superego is involved. When people first learn such rules, they don't necessarily understand the reasons behind them. But later, as they become older, they begin to develop their own ideas about right and wrong. These ideas become part of the superego.

You may be thinking that the superego is the opposite of the id. If so, you are partly right, for there is one similarity that the superego and the id share: Both are unrealistic parts of personality. Neither considers the way the world actually operates.

In the case of the id, it pushes us to fulfill every desire immediately. Obviously, this is unrealistic. On the other hand, the superego propels us towards acting totally perfect all the time. Such a goal is clearly unrealistic, too. Life presents too many roadblocks for people to achieve perfection.

It is up to the ego, then, to step in and act as a referee between the id and the superego. The ego lets people satisfy some of the needs for which the id is pushing. At the same time, it allows the superego to get its way part of the time.

In sum, the operation of the id, ego, and superego combine. It is this combination of these three facets that makes for an individual's unique personality.

HOW PERSONALITY DEVELOPS

Up to now, we have been discussing how Freud's psychoanalytic theory explains personality in adults. But people are not born with fully-formed personalities. Instead, Freud suggests, the various

TABLE 1. The Stages of Personality Development According to Freud's Psychoanalytic Theory

Stage	Age	Major Characteristics
Oral	Birth to 12–18 months	Interest in oral gratification from sucking, eating, mouthing, biting
Anal	12–18 months to 3 years	Gratification from expelling and withholding feces; coming to terms with society's controls relating to toilet training
Phallic	3 to 5–6 years	Interest in the genitals; coming to terms with Oedipal/Electra conflict, leading to identification with same-sex parent
Latency	5–6 years to adolescence	Sexual concerns largely unimportant
Genital	Adolescence to adulthood	Reemergence of sexual interests and establishment of mature sexual relationships

parts of personality slowly emerge as a person ages.

In Freud's view, people move through a series of stages during childhood. During each stage, particular kinds of experiences may affect the unconscious. Because they are in the unconscious, these experiences may affect later behavior, even in adulthood.[3]

Each stage of the development of a child's personality spotlights a different major biological activity. Freud thought that these biological activities were related to how a child experienced pleasure in a particular stage. Each stage is named for its function. (Table 1 summarizes each stage.)

THE ORAL STAGE. The first period of personality formation is the *oral stage.* This stage lasts from birth to twelve to eighteen months.

In the oral stage, a baby's mouth is the center of pleasure. If you've ever seen a baby of this age, you know that babies are always trying to stick anything they can get their hands on into their mouths. They suck, mouth, and bite just about everything.

Freud looked at this behavior and decided that the mouth was the most important location for receiving pleasure at this age. He also thought that adult personality was affected by what happened during the oral stage.

For instance, Freud felt if infants became frustrated by not being fed quickly enough when they were hungry during the oral stage, they might develop future personality problems. But he also felt that future personality difficulties might occur if babies were overly pampered by parents who rushed to feed them as soon as they cried.

What kind of adult personality problems could occur as a result of difficulties in the oral stage? Freud thought that adults would display personality traits related to the mouth. For instance, an adult who talks too much might be showing oral-stage problems. In the same way, eating so much that you get fat or being unable to stop smoking might be behaviors related to difficulties in the oral stage.

THE ANAL STAGE. The next stage in personality development, according to Freud, is the anal stage. It lasts from about twelve to eighteen months until around three years of age.

In this stage, the focus of pleasure shifts from the mouth. Instead, children enjoy more and more the acts of urinating and having bowel movements. They like having control over their elimination.

But it is in this period that their parents begin to toilet-train them. This often marks the start of a battle of wills. Parents try to control their children's chief source of pleasure, and the children resist.

Psychoanalytic theory says that problems during the anal stage can be mirrored in adult personality. For instance, unusual neatness may be caused by stern toilet training during the anal stage. In addition, though, the opposite adult characteristic can be produced in the anal stage: Adults who are unusually messy may be acting that way because of things that happened during their anal stage.

THE PHALLIC STAGE. Around the age of three, children enter the phallic stage. It lasts until about age five or six.

During this stage, a child's chief source of biological pleasure comes from the genitals. Children may touch or stroke themselves. They begin to get some ideas about sex.

As the differences between boys and girls

become more obvious, children may develop a kind of romantic interest in their parent of the opposite sex. This happens toward the end of the phallic stage.

However, because such romance is clearly not reasonable, children try to refocus their energy. They refocus it on their same-sex parent, and they do it through a process called identification. *Identification* is a child's attempt to be similar to his or her same-sex parent.

Identification is important for the development of personality. When they try to be like their same-sex parent, children develop a superego. They form a conscience. Boys learn behavior that society thinks is especially correct for men, and girls learn the same for women.

After the end of the phallic period, several years go by in which not much personality development occurs. This period, lasting from about five or six until around age thirteen, is called the *latency* period.

GENITAL PERIOD. The final period of personality development starts at around the age of thirteen. According to Freud, the *genital period* consists of increasingly adultlike behavior. Both boys and girls begin to focus on getting along with others. They think about marriage and having children of their own.

According to Freud and psychoanalytic theory, personality development is complete at the end of the genital period. Our personalities are fully formed, and we function as adults.

IS FREUD'S PSYCHOANALYTIC EXPLANATION CORRECT?

Freud's psychoanalytic explanation of personality presents a complex view of personality development. It says that the way we act as adults is very much a result of the kind of experiences we have as young children. But is it right?

There is no easy answer to such a question. Some people believe that Freud was mostly wrong. They say that no definite evidence exists that people go through the stages that psychoanalytic theory says they do. Others suggest that the theory is too imprecise to be of much use. For instance, they wonder what good is a theory that predicts that people are very messy or very neat for exactly the same reasons.

Some people even deny the existence of the unconscious. They say that it is not very scientific to talk about things that people are not aware of. They say that scientists shouldn't study things that can't ever be directly observed by others.

On the other hand, many people believe that Freud and psychoanalytic theory actually provide a good explanation of personality. Freud's supporters say that the personality problems of adults can be traced to their difficulties and problems in childhood. They also think the unconscious does exist.

We don't know for sure who is right. But it is clear that Freud and psychoanalysis are important. They have had an impact on all other explanations of personality. What is especially important is the idea that we have a hidden part of personality, the unconscious, that helps direct our behavior. This is an idea that Freud was the first to discuss, and it is a profound contribution to our understanding of personality.

CHAPTER TWO

Humanism and Behaviorism

Kenny spent the first three years of his life in a hospital and a children's home. His mother had deserted him. He has AIDS.

If Gertrude Lewis hadn't come along, he probably never would have lived in a real home. Gertrude was a volunteer in the children's home where Kenny was living as an orphan. She was forty-seven years old, and she didn't have a family of her own.

Then Gertrude met Kenny. "I saw this boy with these beautiful eyes," she remembers, "just looking up and smiling." It was love at first sight. She decided to become Kenny's foster mother.

Kenny now lives with Gertrude, and both are happy. Sadly, the happiness is temporary. Because Kenny has AIDS, Gertrude understands he will get sick and die. But knowing he has AIDS makes every moment even more important (Gibbs, 1989).

Anyone looking at Gertrude Lewis would see a personality that is generous, warm, and open. She took a child into her life who has no future. His last days of life will be happy because of her.

Where does such a personality come from? Freud and psychoanalysis, which we talked about in the last chapter, would say that it was Gertrude's unconscious that led her to act the way she did. In other words, experiences she had when she was a young child led her to develop unconscious urges to act in a generous way.

However, there are other ways of explaining her generosity and kindness. Some experts in personality say that we should be looking at entirely different reasons to explain personality.

In this chapter, we'll look at two different explanations for personality. The first is called humanism. Humanism explains personality by saying that people are basically good and that human beings usually act in a positive way.

The second explanation, called behaviorism, says that personality develops through rewards and punishments. If someone acts generously, for example, it is just because they have been rewarded for doing so in the past. It is not because they are fundamentally good.

As we'll see, these two explanations are not only very different from one another, they are also quite different from psychoanalysis. We'll begin with humanism.

HUMANISM: LOOKING AT THE POSITIVE IN PEOPLE

Consider the great artist Michelangelo. The heroism of firefighters and police officers. The giving Mother Teresa, who helps the poor in Calcutta, India. What is it that makes such people so admirable?

According to *humanistic* explanations of personality, people like this are showing a basic goodness. This goodness is a part of a human being, and it can be found in everyone. In some people, their positive qualities have already come to the surface. In others, though, it is more hidden. Humanistic explanations say that we all have positive qualities at the core of our personalities. In some of us, these positive qualities are more visible than in others.

Why don't all people show their underlying good qualities? One answer is that they first have to take care of more immediate needs. According to one personality expert, Abraham Maslow, we must first take care of our basic needs that have to do with life and death.[1] For example, we need to have enough water, food, and sleep in order to

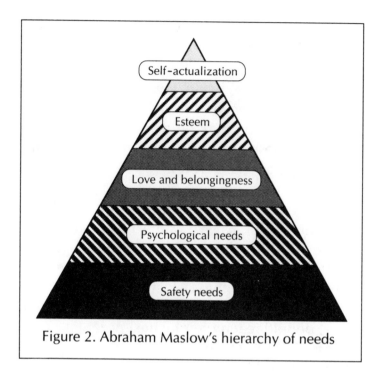

Figure 2. Abraham Maslow's hierarchy of needs

live. If we don't satisfy these kinds of needs, it is not likely that we'd be able to display more humane kinds of behavior.

Maslow goes further in his thinking. He says that there is a progression of stages that people pass through in order to reach their highest levels of behavior.

We can look at these stages as a triangle, illustrated in Figure 2. As you can see basic biological needs that must be taken care of are at the bottom.

Once these needs are provided, we then become concerned about our safety. We need a secure place to live, one where we don't have to worry about our personal protection.

At the next stage, says Maslow, we need to be concerned about being loved. Maslow thinks everyone wants to be loved and to belong to a group. The group may be made up of family or friends. It doesn't matter—we all need to feel that we are part of some group.

Needing to be seen by others in a positive way makes up the next stage. We want to know that others value us. We want to feel that we are respected, that others hold us in high regard.

If we make it this far up the triangle, we may eventually reach the last stage. This stage is called *self-actualization.* In the self-actualization stage, people reach their highest potential. They become the best person they are capable of being.

For instance, suppose you are a person who has unusual artistic talents. If you were to become self-actualized, you would be able to display your artistic talents fully. You would fulfill everything that you are capable of. Or suppose your main talent was in teaching other people. If you become self-actualized, you would have the opportunity to teach, and you would be an extraordinary teacher.

According to Maslow, it is not so important what your particular talent is. What is important is that you feel satisfied with what you do and that you do a good job at it.

The lives of people who are self-actualized

are rich and full. But self-actualization doesn't result in perfection. People who are self-actualized sometimes get angry or are stubborn. Still, self-actualization is a goal to aim for.

Humanistic explanations say that everyone has the chance to be self-actualized. Then why do some people fulfill this potential, while others don't?

The answer is that some people live in a situation that doesn't allow them to fulfill the lower stages of the triangle. If they can't achieve the lower parts of the triangle, then they can't reach the higher stages.

But there is another reason that some people don't become self-actualized. It is not easy to be self-actualized, because it is necessary to know ourselves very well. If we are to reach our full potential, we must have an idea what that potential is. We must also learn what our potential is not, and learning this can be painful.

For instance, suppose you always wanted to be a professional athlete. But also suppose that you really don't have the talent. If that is true, finding out that you don't have what it takes may be painful. But this awareness is necessary for you to become self-actualized in some other area. You'll need to learn what your actual talents are so that you can reach your potential in the area where your real talents lie.

In sum, humanistic explanations of personality focus on the positive in people. They say that all people are basically good. What makes one person different from another is how much they are able to display this goodness.

However, not everyone agrees with this view. Some critics of humanistic explanations say that it is not scientific to assume that all people are good. They say that it is impossible to prove that humans have the underlying positive qualities that humanistic explanations say they do. Instead of assuming that humans have this underlying goodness, these theories say we should be looking for explanations that don't assume some special, positive qualities. Instead, they say we should look outside of the person to explain personality. This kind of explanation is called behaviorism.

BEHAVIORISM: LOOKING AT SURFACE BEHAVIOR

Let's go back to the story of Gertrude Lewis, the woman who took in a baby with AIDS as a foster child. Why did she do it?

A humanistic explanation of personality would say that she is basically a good person. But if we used behaviorism, the explanation would be different.

A behavioristic explanation would look at the enjoyment Gertrude would get from taking care of the baby. It would point to the praise she would get from her friends for taking in the child. It would consider how she would feel good about helping someone in need.

In short, behaviorism would look at the

rewards Gertrude would receive for her behavior. It would not look for personal traits or say that she is basically a good person. Instead, it would ignore what's inside her. It would concentrate on how she has learned that some kinds of behavior— such as acting generously—are likely to lead to certain rewards.

Behaviorism is an explanation of personality that focuses on observable behavior.[2] It proposes that we shouldn't worry about the inner workings of the mind. Instead, we should concentrate on how circumstances and events in a person's life have taught that person to act in a certain way.

Those who believe that behaviorism explains a person's personality would say that our person-alities are the sum of all the behaviors we have learned. Some of us have learned to act gener-ously; others have learned to behave selfishly.

People don't differ in their behavior because they are basically good or bad inside. Instead, their personalities are shaped by what they have learned about how to act.

For instance, suppose someone is usually friendly at school and at parties. Behaviorism would say that they have been previously rewarded for being friendly in both situations. Because of these past rewards, they are more likely to be friendly in other situations, too.

Behaviorism also says that we learn the behaviors that make up our personalities by observing others.[3] By watching the rewards peo-ple receive by behaving in some way, we are more likely to try out the behavior ourselves. Similarly, we may see someone who is punished for behaving in one kind of way. We are less likely to behave in the same way ourselves in the future.

For example, suppose a young boy sees a television show where an actor gets his way by picking a fight with someone. Because the actor ends up getting what he wants, we can say that the actor has been rewarded for fighting.

After observing the violence that has been rewarded on TV, a child who watched the show later might be more likely to pick a fight in the future. If this happens a lot, we may say that the boy has developed an aggressive personality. In other words, he learns that aggressive behavior is rewarded.

Behaviorism doesn't pay much attention to what's inside a person. It examines only how a person behaves. If people act irritably, they are said to have learned to have an irritable personality. If they act honestly, they are said to have learned to have an honest personality.

If you want to change people's personality, behaviorism says, you need to teach them new behaviors. They don't need to change their understanding of the world; it is enough to teach them to behave differently.

The behaviorism explanation of personality has many critics. These critics object to the basic view of behaviorism: that we shouldn't care about the inner person. They say that people are special in some way. They also argue that personality is more than just a bundle of learned behaviors.

Finally, critics of behaviorism say that it sees people in the wrong light. They think that people are more in control of their own behavior than behaviorism would suggest. They say that people's behavior is not shaped only by things that they learn. Instead, they say, we have a lot of control over our lives. To sum up, critics say that humanism is a better explanation of personality than is behaviorism.

The debate between humanism and behaviorism has not been won by either side. Some people feel that one is more correct than the other, and others feel the opposite. And some people feel that both are wrong; they say that psychoanalysis is a better explanation than the other two.

We can't say for sure which is correct. In some ways, it is not even too useful to ask which is right. Since each explanation looks at somewhat different parts of personality, each makes different assumptions. So to ask which is right is not a totally reasonable question.

Some experts in personality have turned away from all three of these explanations. Instead, they have tried to explain personality by identifying the most basic qualities, or traits, that make one person different from another. We'll discuss traits next.

CHAPTER THREE

Traits: The Labels of Personality

"Who are you going to vote for in the class elections, Juan?" asked Greta.

"I'm not sure," responded Juan. "Ellie is really hardworking, and she gets things done. But I just wonder about her bossiness. She's always telling people what to do, and sometimes she can be annoying."

"I know what you mean," said Greta. "So you're going to vote for Hank?"

"Well, I'm not sure about that. Hank is pretty smart, but he seems so laid back and relaxed that I'm not sure that he'll ever get anything accomplished. I really don't know. There are some things about both of them I like, and some things about both of them I dislike."

Hardworking. Bossy. Annoying. Smart. Laid back. Relaxed.

When we look back at the conversation between Juan and Greta, we find that their descriptions of Hank are made up of a series of traits. Most of us use traits in our descriptions of others' personalities. We often try to recognize the most important or meaningful traits to figure out why people behave as they do.

Some experts in personality have taken a similar approach. They have tried to identify the most basic and fundamental personality characteristics, which they call traits. *Traits* are lasting aspects of personality that differentiate one person from another.

When using traits to explain personality, we do not assume that some people have a trait and that others do not. For instance, a personality explanation using traits would not say that one person has a "friendliness" trait and that others do not have a "friendliness" trait.

Instead, we would say that all people have the same basic set of traits. However, people are different in how much the trait applies to them. For example, it might be that everyone has a "friendliness" trait. It is just that some people are high in "friendliness," and others are low in it.

The most important question that trait explanations of personality have to answer is this: What are the most basic and fundamental traits? As we shall see, different experts have come to very different conclusions.

GORDON ALLPORT'S CARDINAL TRAITS

One way of finding out how many traits there are is to look in a dictionary. One personality expert, Gordon Allport, did just that, but he found so many traits that he was overwhelmed. Listed in the dictionary were around eighteen thousand separate traits. Even after he combined words that had the same meaning, he was left with close to five thousand separate trait descriptions.

Obviously, this kind of list was too long to be of much help in determining what were the most basic traits. After studying the traits, Allport decided that they could be divided into three categories. The three categories of traits he found were: cardinal, central, and secondary.[1]

Allport said that a *cardinal trait* was a single personality characteristic that guides most of an individual's day-to-day activities. For example, if we have the cardinal trait of "helpfulness," almost everything we do would be directed toward being helpful to others. On the other hand, someone who had the cardinal trait of "greediness" would spend almost every waking moment trying to become wealthy.

However, most of us do not have a cardinal trait that directs all our behavior. Instead, we have a small group of central traits. These central traits make up the core of our personalities. *Central traits* are our main personality characteristics. When we describe others, we usually use central traits to talk about them. For instance, when discussing Hank, Juan and Greta used such central traits as "smart" and "relaxed."

Finally, Allport said that the third category of traits were secondary traits. *Secondary traits* are the least important personality characteristics. They are traits that influence a person's behavior only in certain situations. In some ways they are similar to particular likes or dislikes. For example, our preference for horror movies might be thought of as a secondary trait.

USING MATHEMATICS TO IDENTIFY BASIC TRAITS

Allport's suggestion to divide traits into three basic types was helpful. However, it still did not answer the primary question of trait explanations: Which specific traits are the most important?

To try to answer this question more precisely, other experts in personality have taken a different approach from Allport's. These experts have tried to use mathematical techniques to decide what traits are most important.

In this approach, a mathematical technique called factor analysis is used. *Factor analysis* is a way of combining traits into broader, more general patterns. Researchers use factor analysis to identify which personality traits are linked together in people. The mathematics involved are so complex that computers are used to do the calculations.

Specifically, a personality researcher interested in using factor analysis would first ask a large group of people to fill out a survey questionnaire. Each person would be given a long list of traits and asked to indicate which of the traits would most apply to them.

The answers then would be fed into a computer for the factor analysis to be calculated. In factor analysis, the computer can determine what groups of traits are found together in the same person. It can also see what traits separate one person from another. Finally, the computer can tell if there is some pattern or overall combination of traits that go together.

Depending on who does the factor analysis, different sets of primary traits have been found. But why hasn't just one set of traits been identified?

The answer is that not everyone measures traits in the same way. For instance, different studies may use questionnaires that use different words in asking people questions about what traits are important to them. As a result, the information that is fed into the computer is different, depending on which personality expert is doing the research.

In addition, not every computer program doing factor analysis does it in exactly the same way. Therefore, the actual mathematical calculations used in factor analysis may differ from one researcher to another. For these reasons, personality researchers using factor analysis have come up with different sets of primary traits.

CATTELL'S FACTOR ANALYSIS EXPLANATION OF PERSONALITY. One of the most important personality experts is Raymond Cattell. He thinks that there are sixteen source traits. *Source traits* are the basic units of personality. For Cattell, these sixteen traits make up the core of personality.[2]

Cattell thinks that all people have the same sixteen source traits. For instance, one trait refers to how serious a person is. Some people are very serious; others are happy-go-lucky; and most lie somewhere in between.

In order to measure these sixteen personality traits, Cattell has developed a questionnaire called the "Sixteen Personality Factor Questionnaire," or the "16 PF" for short.

The 16 PF gives a score for each of the sixteen traits. It is also possible to combine the results of groups of people. For instance, the graph in Figure 3 shows how airline pilots and writers score, on average. As you can see, the two groups have a very different pattern of results. What this means, of course, is that airline pilots and writers tend to have different kinds of personalities.

EYSENCK'S FACTOR ANALYSIS EXPLANATION OF PERSONALITY. Not everyone agrees with Cattell that there are sixteen personality traits. When other personality researchers do factor analyses, they come up with a different number of traits. One of those who differs most from Cattell is Hans Eysenck.[3]

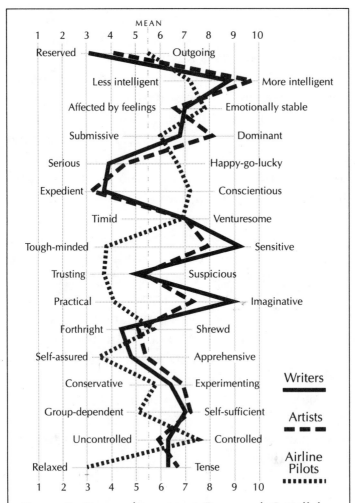

Figure 3. Personality expert Raymond Cattell has developed a list of sixteen pairs of "source traits," shown to the left and right of the graph. In one study, three groups of subjects—writers, creative artists, and airline pilots—were tested for these traits. Would you have been able to predict these results? *(Reprinted by permission of the Institute for Personality and Ability Testing.)*

Although he also used factor analysis, Eysenck concluded that the personality could be described in terms of just two different traits, or "dimensions." The first major personality dimension involves how extroverted people are. For instance, you probably know people who are outgoing, friendly, and open. These people are *extroverted.* On the other hand, you probably also have met people who are quiet, careful, and thoughtful. These people are just the opposite from extroverted; they are *introverted.* Eysenck thinks that the amount that people are extroverted is one of the two major personality characteristics.

Eysenck's second major personality trait has to do with how stable people are. Some people are calm, reliable, and even-tempered most of the time. These people are relatively *stable.* But others are just the opposite. They are moody, touchy, and sensitive much of the time. He calls these people *neurotic.*

THE "BIG FIVE" PERSONALITY TRAITS. We've now looked at two major explanations of personality that rely on factor analysis. You might be surprised to learn that there are quite a few other researchers doing factor analysis. The number of basic traits they find ranges from three to seven.

No one is sure how many basic traits there really are, but a good deal of recent research says that there are five. These are so important that they are sometimes called the "Big Five" personality traits.

These are the "Big Five" personality traits: extroversion, neuroticism, intellect, agreeableness, and conscientiousness.[4] It is interesting to see that the first two traits are on Eysenck's list. It is also interesting that the last three traits are similar to ones found in Cattell's list of the sixteen source traits. Even though different experts find different sets of traits, they seem to be measuring much the same thing.

THE TROUBLE WITH TRAITS

Trait explanations of personality have a lot going for them. They fit our everyday ideas of what makes up personality. Remember, for example, the conversation at the start of the chapter, which consisted of a series of trait descriptions. Traits give us a way of looking at other people and comparing them with each other.

But trait explanations of personality also have drawbacks. For one thing, each time experts try to make a list of the primary traits, they come up with a different conclusion. Are there sixteen major traits? Two? Five? The number changes, depending upon whom you ask.

Even more important is this: What is it that traits actually help us explain? Traits are really only labels or descriptions. They do not explain why people develop particular traits in the first place. They don't tell us how personality changes as people get older. They don't give information about how traits influence behavior. They just give us labels.

In sum, some experts believe that traits, by themselves, don't explain very much. But even these experts wouldn't say that traits have no use. Some personality experts feel that traits are important when we consider them along with particular kinds of situations.

For example, some kinds of situations might make an introverted person behave one way. At the same time, the same situation might make an extroverted person behave another way. The person's traits and the situation work together to produce behavior. Learning about traits, then, can help us to understand better why people behave as they do.

PART TWO

—WHEN—
PERSONALITY
—GOES—
WRONG

CHAPTER FOUR

Personality Disorders

We've seen how people's traits can be used to describe how they most often behave with other people and the world. In one sense, personality traits determine how people manage, or cope, most of the time. They also affect how people see and understand themselves.

Traits can be adaptive or maladaptive. Traits that are *adaptive* help people accomplish their work and get along with others. To be adaptive, traits must be flexible. This means that they must allow a person to change how he or she behaves according to the situation. For example, it is reasonable to be aggressive if you are playing football. But it is not wise to be aggressive when you have to cooperate on a project at school.

What if people's traits become so inflexible that they don't let them fit into what they are required to do in order to be successful in their work? What happens if their personal quirks or habits become so irritating to others that they are unable to form good relationships? In this situation, the traits are considered maladaptive. *Maladaptive* traits hinder people's relationships and work.

In some cases, personality traits are so maladaptive that they interfere with a person's ability to adjust to many different social and personal situations. In these cases, they represent what mental health professionals call a *personality disorder.*[1]

TYPES OF PERSONALITY DISORDERS

Mental health professionals have identified several types and categories of personality disorders.[2] Some of these disorders describe people who are unusually afraid and nervous. Another category includes the disorders that impair people's functioning in a way that they seem odd and unusual. The final category of disorders includes people who are too emotional, unpredictable, unreliable, and difficult to have around. One of these disorders describes people who are actually dangerous to others.

We will discuss each of these categories next. However, before we proceed, you should know that although people with personality disorders are limited in their ability to get along with others in some ways (sometimes very seriously), they are still usually able to hold their jobs and live with their families. They do not hear voices or see Martians, and they are aware (sometimes too aware!) of how other people are behaving.

DISORDERS THAT MAKE PEOPLE APPEAR AFRAID AND NERVOUS. Everyone seems to know someone whose personality traits make them so difficult to be around they would do almost anything to avoid them. Sometimes it's clear what you don't like. Sometimes it's more difficult to know.

Consider this case:

> *Jose and Lois are in the junior high cafeteria, talking about the social studies project they are supposed to be working on with Rick. Lois is uncomfortable, and finally says to Jose that she can't stand trying to work with Rick.*
>
> *"It's not that Rick isn't smart, or that he's obnoxious," Lois tells Jose. "He knows how to talk to people. It's just that he's always arguing about the smallest details. He can't joke and relax and he's always insisting that they have to check everything they write a million times and do things his way most of the time. He's just no fun to be around."*
>
> *Jose agrees and remembers when he made the mistake of inviting Rick along to a movie. They ended up late and missed the beginning because Rick couldn't leave home until he made sure a dozen times*

that he turned off his computer and his radio and put his clothes away in just the right spot.

It might seem to you that Rick was just being serious, careful, and taking charge. However, suppose Rick became more and more serious so that he almost never had fun and was always concerned with work. Suppose he also got more and more careful so that he became a perfectionist and couldn't get anything done on time and seemed always to be thinking about his work. And suppose he took charge so much that he would not let others work in their own ways, and could not cooperate with others on projects or activities because he was afraid that they would not do it right. Furthermore, what if Rick also became so concerned with saving things that he wouldn't throw away even his junk, and he wouldn't give other people things he no longer needed?

If Rick showed all these traits (and perhaps some others we have not mentioned) most of the time, for many years into his twenties, he might have a type of emotional problem called an obsessive-compulsive personality disorder. People with an *obsessive-compulsive personality disorder* are so serious, so interested in details, and so convinced that they need to be in control that they are just no fun to be around. People with this problem not only can't cooperate with others, but they also can't really get anything accomplished themselves.

Now consider this example:

Ellen would really like to get to know James, one of her classmates, better. He seems smart, sensitive, and different from the other kids in her class. He doesn't seem to have too many friends, but she thinks he might be able to relate to her. She's started a few conversations between classes that were promising. She thought he was just shy most of the time.

Taking a chance, she recently asked him to work on a duet together for chorus and he agreed after a lot of hesitation. But when she showed up a few minutes late for their meeting, he seemed to withdraw into a shell. From then on, it was hard to get him to say much of anything. He seemed overly concerned about what her being late meant. He took it personally as a rejection and it reminded him of times that other people seemed to dump him. He became more and more shy and hesitant.

In this example, it is possible that James might just be hesitant and shy around Ellen. But suppose that he always acted that way with almost every other person, and he still showed this kind of behavior even when he was an adult. Suppose he never tried to let others get to know him, and he avoided almost every social event unless he was absolutely certain he'd be liked. Suppose, too, that he always thought that he'd be rejected and had little self-confidence as a result.

One explanation for such behavior is that James might have what could be called an *avoidant personality disorder*. A person with this problem would have no close friends or buddies except perhaps someone in his or her family. He or she might be afraid of being embarrassed or of saying the wrong thing. People with this disorder might hang back more and more. They might miss out on getting to know how to get along with other people because they were convinced they couldn't take a chance on letting people know them.

DISORDERS THAT MAKE PEOPLE SEEM ODD OR UNUSUAL. Have you ever heard someone say that someone else is paranoid? What they probably meant was that the person seems unusually and unreasonably suspicious. People who are paranoid think that others are "out to get them" as a result of even the smallest indication that they are being insulted.

If a paranoid person saw two friends talking to each other, and they did not say hello, the person might think that he was being ignored on purpose. If his or her name was misspelled on an invitation or a team listing, a paranoid person might think that the writer of the invitation or the coach was being nasty. If this suspicious trait lasted and grew more extreme over many years, the person might have what is called a *paranoid personality disorder.*

People with paranoid personality disorder cannot trust others. They are always looking for evidence that they are being ignored, slighted, or taken advantage of. Because they are looking so hard for this evidence, they usually find it. They misinterpret the normal and innocent mistakes of others as a plot against them. Because they can't trust and are always misinterpreting the meaning of others' behavior, they don't make very good friends. They don't become good partners or spouses. Eventually people give up on them. Their own suspiciousness prevents them from keeping good friends and being happy with others.

But even though people with a paranoid personality disorder can't form good relationships with others, they don't usually seek the help of a counselor. Why? Because they believe everyone else is to blame for their problems, and even if they did ask for help, they'd probably end up believing that the counselor was against them too.

DISORDERS THAT MAKE PEOPLE TOO EMOTIONAL, DIFFICULT, AND UNRELIABLE. Some people seem to feel that they are the most important people in the world. They think they are "owed" an unusual amount of attention, respect, and love for their abilities. They seem to think that people should adore them just for existing.

These are people who go beyond being "stuck up." They've showed these characteristics for many years. While they may feel that they are great to be around, they are actually very poor friends because they are so self-centered. It's not so much that they are suspicious (as a person with a paranoid personality would be). It's more that they don't seem to have what it takes to understand others' feelings.

People with this set of personality characteristics are said to have a *narcissistic personality disorder.* The name "narcissistic" comes from the ancient Greek myth of Narcissus. In the myth, Narcissus fell in love with himself after seeing his reflection in a pool.

Usually people with a narcissistic personality disorder will have had many relationships with other people that break up. They will find that they have no real, close friends. Eventually, such people might seek the help of a counselor or therapist. If they are to be really helped, a counselor would have to bring them to understand and experience the feelings of others. Experiencing the feelings of other people is called empathy, and it's the very trait that people with a narcissistic personality disorder lack.

As a final example of a personality disorder, you probably have read stories or seen television accounts of people who seem to care nothing for human life and who display no hint of a conscience. They don't seem to feel guilt or anxiety about the illegal and unethical things they do, and they've been doing such things since at least before age fifteen. They are sometimes people who appear to be quite interesting, even charming, at first. But they later turn out to be liars who will often act with great cruelty and take advantage of others.

People with personalities like this don't live up to their responsibilities to others on the job or at home. They often take careless chances at a moment's notice. If they feel like doing something, they usually do it without thinking of the consequences and without carefully planning what they are trying to accomplish. (This is one of the things that distinguishes them from "normal" criminals who carefully try to get away with what they do.)

They may be people who have never had a career other than picking on their victims or, surprisingly, they may be "successful" business people who steal retirement money from unsuspecting older people. They also may be very aggressive and irritable with others.

People who display this type of behavior are said to have *antisocial personality disorder.* A person with antisocial personality disorder is characterized by having no apparent conscience and no regard for the pain and suffering of others or for the moral and ethical standards of society. These traits make people with this disorder dangerous to the individuals they come in contact with and to society in general.

"ORDINARY" PROBLEM OR PERSONALITY DISORDER? You'll notice that we used the words "might have" when we talked about the first few disorders. It's important to be able to distinguish between the normal problems and anxieties of everyday living and what we are calling a personality disorder. By now you might be thinking that you, or someone close to you, has had some of these problems. You might even think that these problems could be called a personality disorder. How do we know when a problem is just a problem (the kind anyone might expect to encounter in their lives) and when it represents a disorder (a mental or emotional disorder)?

It's quite normal for most people to find themselves in situations where they don't adjust well from time to time. But some people's traits keep them from adjusting almost all the time. In addition, they don't adjust in most of the social and personal situations in which they find themselves. When this happens, it may be that they have a personality disorder.

In other words, deciding on whether a person has a personality disorder depends on how serious problems are and how often they occur. Just as in Chapter 1 we said that consistency in behavior is part of personality, it is also true that traits that are consistently maladaptive from situation to situation and from time to time define a personality disorder. It is the person's inflexible and maladaptive style and pattern of behaving that is described by the term personality disorder. They make the person unable to adapt at work and at home.

It's important to realize that to diagnose a personality disorder, a mental health professional must have evidence that the person's inflexible and troubled approach to life has existed for a long time. For adults, this evidence can be found by looking back over their personal, social, and work life for many years. But for teenagers, who are still developing an approach to life, it is more difficult to be certain that the consistency of troubling personality traits has existed long enough to call it a personality disorder. As a result, the distinction between normal and abnormal personality traits (which is often quite difficult to decide upon anyway) is even more difficult to make for teenagers. So although the traits that make up a personality disorder may actually begin in the teenage years, it's hard actually to say that a teenager has a personality disorder.

WHO FEELS TROUBLED—THE PERSON OR THE PEOPLE AROUND THE PERSON? Sometimes personality disorders produce a sense of frustration and distress to the person affected. In some cases, however, individuals do not feel any sense of distress. Rather, it is the people around them who feel distress.

In one of our first examples in this chapter, Ellen wanted to begin a relationship with James. But he felt rejected by her lateness. He thought that she was really not interested in him. Unfortunately, this had happened before to James. He thought others had rejected him, and he was sad and resentful that this happened so often.

James, though, didn't know what to do. He didn't know that he could try to get help and change. People with these disorders often see their own personality, and the world they live in, as unchangeable. Because of this, they don't seek help for their disorders.

On the other hand, Jose and Lois seemed to end up feeling the distress of trying to interact with someone whose personality traits made him very hard to get along with. When counselors work with people with personality disorders, it is often not the people with the disorder who originate the counseling. Rather, it may be a friend or relative who is worried and "sends" those with the problem to the counselor.

Unfortunately, the individuals with the disorder may feel that it is *others* whose behavior is difficult. As a result of this misperception, they may not see the pattern of difficulties in their relationship with the world. They may feel that others are to blame, and refuse to get the help they need.

CHAPTER FIVE

When One Is Not Enough: Multiple Personality Disorder

Think how you'd react if one day you read a newspaper article about a man found guilty of forcing a twenty-seven-year-old woman to have sex. The article says that only one woman was on the witness stand during the trial. But then the story goes on to say that the prosecutor put six women on the witness stand to accuse the man.

The explanation? The woman had a psychological disorder called *multiple personality disorder.* When that one woman "blinked her eyes" and "bowed her head" on the stand, six different personalities then came out and testified.[1] One of them was a six-year-old girl. Another was a twenty-year-old who did not know what sex was.

As a result of her testimony, the jury found the man guilty. They believed he took advantage of the twenty year old by talking her into having sex even though she did not know what it was. How did they know this? From the six-year-old!

It used to be that multiple personality disorder was considered extremely rare. Cases like this are now being seen more often than ever before. Although it is unlikely that you will ever meet anyone with such a problem, doctors, lawyers, and mental health workers are all beginning to hear this kind of story a bit more often.

MULTIPLE PERSONALITY DISORDER: WHAT IT IS AND WHAT IT ISN'T

Technically, multiple personality is not really a personality disorder. It is something called a *dissociative* (dih-so-see-a-tive) *disorder.* Dissociative disorders cause parts of an individual's personality to split apart, or "dissociate," from the control of the person. That is why multiple personality disorder used to be called "split personality."

But sometimes it's more than just a part of a personality that is split off. You remember that we talked about personality as the long-lasting traits that determine how people behave and feel about themselves. If some of these traits plus some memories, feelings, and ideas that go with them get split off, whole new personalities can be "created." The result is a multiple personality. In the case at the beginning of this chapter, the new personalities created included the twenty-year-old

68

who did not know about sex and the six-year-old girl. It was as if the parts of the twenty-seven-year-old woman that did not want to know about sex became a twenty-year-old woman. And the child-like feelings of the twenty-seven-year-old became the six-year-old girl.

In multiple personality disorder, when the personality splits apart, it creates others which then take turns controlling the person's life. One person ends up with several distinct (different) personalities. Each one of them has its own consistent way of behaving and feeling. Sometimes there may be only two personalities. More often there are many. Cases with over a hundred different personalities have been reported. In fact, in about half of all cases reported there are more than ten personalities[2]—more than enough for a baseball team!

Regardless of how many additional personalities a person has, each of the personalities can have its own special skills and abilities. One personality might have a high IQ, while another might not know how to read. They might have different habits, memories, and feelings. Different personalities may have their own facial expressions and ways of speaking. They may say that they are male or female. They may say that they have different ages (and act those ages). Sometimes they may speak different languages.

Even more surprising, each personality may have its own different physical abilities or limitations. For instance, one personality might need eyeglasses while another might not.[3] Having different traits means that one personality might be very friendly while another could be very shy and alone. Or one could be very easy to get along with and another could be very angry most of the time.

Finally, some of the personalities could seem quite "normal" while others might appear to have mental problems. This last statement may be confusing, since it would seem that anyone with more than one personality must have a mental disorder. What this means is that if the "normal" personality was in a separate person, that person might seem well-adjusted.

HOW MULTIPLE PERSONALITIES CONTROL A SINGLE BODY

Because there is only one body, the different personalities must have some way of "taking turns" being in control. How do they do this? Usually, there are at least two personalities that take "full control" of the person's life.[4] They are called the "dominant" ones. They may simply take turns with each other and this pattern is called "alternating personality.[5]" Each one, however, may not know what happens when the other is in control.

Sometimes, there are several "subordinate" personalities in addition to the dominant ones.[6] The subordinate ones are usually not in control much but they may be there, "under the surface." They can see everything that the dominant ones are doing. They can then "come out" (take control) and tell what's been going on while they've "been inside" (out of the person's control).

An example of this occurred in a famous case described in a book titled *The Three Faces of Eve.*[7] The book tells of a woman with three personalities. Eve White was the first personality. She was quiet and shy. Eve Black was the other, dominant one. She was the opposite of Eve White— aggressive, outgoing, and getting into trouble often. When Eve Black came out, Eve White would not know it. All she knew was that she had a blackout. Later on, when Eve White was getting help from a therapist, a third personality came out. Her name was Jane. She knew nothing about her life before she came out. She was, however, more responsible and mature than the other two and was probably responsible for trying to put Eve's life back together.

As in the case of *The Three Faces of Eve,* multiple personalities are often opposites of each other. They sometimes come out when a particular problem comes up. Sometimes they come out in seconds. Other times, it may take several minutes.[8] For example, if a timid personality is in control and someone starts to pick on him or her, an angry, aggressive personality might come out to fight back. As with Eve White, the timid personality might come back when the fight is over. Usually, the timid one will not know what happened.

MULTIPLE PERSONALITY DISORDER AND AMNESIA

There is another type of dissociative disorder called psychogenic amnesia. The word *psychogenic* (sy-ko-jen-ik) means caused by the mind. The word *amnesia* (am-knee-sha) means memory loss. Put together they mean the kind of memory loss that's caused by something someone feels or is upset by. (Other kinds of memory loss can be caused by something physical—like getting hit on the head). Amnesia helps to explain how multiple personality disorder might be caused. Amnesia shows us that something very upsetting can change an important part of personality, like memory. It also helps to explain how one personality might not know what another personality has done, by having amnesia for the time the other personality was in control.

Memory is something that is usually just a part of someone's personality. When a person gets amnesia, some (but not all) memory is "lost." We think they only lose the memory of something that upset them. For example, some survivors of natural disasters (like earthquakes) and human disasters (like mass killings) who "get" amnesia can't remember what happened. But they are able to remember what has happened since the event (so they have not lost their brain's ability to remember—it's purely a psychological problem). Why does this happen? One theory is that it happens because our minds try to protect us from hurtful feelings that these memories might cause. If you can't remember, you can't feel hurt.

The personalities that would be upset by traits that frighten them (for example, fighting would upset a timid personality) might get amnesia for the time that they "are inside." Personalities may also get amnesia or become confused so as to avoid feeling "crazy."[9]

THE ORIGINS OF MULTIPLE PERSONALITY

Nobody knows for sure how multiple personality disorder develops. However, there are some strong possibilities. The one that is most discussed lately explains multiple personality as the result of horrible abuse or stress. In order to protect oneself from the pain, the person splits apart into multiple personalities.

One recent case illustrates this theory.[10] Juanita was a woman who was in jail for bank robbery. But she said she didn't do it. Instead, she said, it was done by one of her other personalities.

According to the story, Juanita was tortured with beatings when she was a young child by her mother, who was an alcoholic. She was sold to men for money before she was ten years old. She was then kidnapped by three men and raped when she was fourteen. Her life was so horrible that, in the words of one reporter, "she dropped out of her own life and created others to share an ordeal she could not bear alone."

Juanita had seven other personalities, and

each one of them had a specific "job." Jennifer was an extrovert (someone who is very outgoing and sociable). Ann appeared to want to mother Juanita's children, but she was depressed. Linda was "the brains" of the group. She knew a lot about law and psychiatry. (You could see where that would be useful to Juanita!) Anna was an eight-year-old girl who was angry about not getting taken care of. Tricia was the personality who took care of her body; she jogged and worked out. Susan was "the peacemaker"—another useful personality for Juanita's life. And finally, there was a personality called Wanda Westin. Wanda was the first to split off. Her function was to be the "protector." She came out early, when Juanita was two or three years old, to "take the abuse Juanita could not handle."

As an adult, Juanita first got into serious trouble when Wanda killed a woman in a motel where Juanita was working as a chambermaid. While she was working in a room, Wanda came out and killed the woman. Apparently, Wanda then went back inside and Juanita continued working. She made no attempt to get away because she did not know what was going on. She was arrested and sent to a state mental hospital where she was given the diagnosis of multiple personality disorder. She was then put on trial.

With Juanita on the witness stand, Wanda was called to testify. She admitted that she killed the woman. Juanita was then called to testify. All she could say was that "they say I killed someone.

I have to take their word for it." She was found not guilty by reason of insanity and sent back to the state mental hospital where she stayed for eight years.

TREATING MULTIPLE PERSONALITY DISORDER

Many different ideas exist for the treatment of multiple personality disorder. The case of Juanita can be used to explain some ideas about what does, and does not, help.

When Juanita was first sent to a state mental hospital, she was given strong drugs to keep her calm. The doctors also thought these drugs (called major tranquilizers) would keep the different personalities from surfacing again. During the eight years she was in the hospital, doctors told her that Wanda had to be removed. However, they were unsuccessful. The drugs only made it so that, in Juanita's words, "we could hardly function." Obviously, the drugs did not make the additional personalities disappear.

Instead, Juanita's therapists now think that the undesired personalities actually just "submerged" (just as a submarine goes under the water to avoid being seen and destroyed). They went inside and did not come out during the rest of the time in the hospital. However, they were not gone.

Juanita was released from the hospital, supposedly improved. But during this time, Wanda had not disappeared; she was just hiding. After

Juanita's release, Wanda came out. She robbed a bank, and Juanita was arrested again. Rather than going back to the hospital, she chose to go to jail. She said that at least that way, she would not have to take the drugs any longer. Juanita also hoped that by letting the personalities come out, she eventually would be made whole again. She said that she wanted to take responsibility for who she was. In jail, she communicated with all of the personalities every day.

THE CONFUSIONS OF MULTIPLE PERSONALITY

As you can see, multiple personality raises many questions for people other than those who suffer from it. For example, if one of the personalities commits a crime, should all of them pay for it by going to jail or to a mental hospital? Should people with multiple personality be held responsible for their behavior? Can people "use" the disorder to avoid punishment? Do some people develop multiple personality just because their doctors and the rest of us find it so interesting? We are still not sure of all the answers to these questions.

By the way, don't think that multiple personality always convinces juries to let people go. Consider a case from the city of Lowell, Massachusetts.[11] A woman on trial for selling drugs claimed that she should not be held responsible for her actions because she had multiple personality disorder. The jury found her guilty!

76

PART THREE

UNMASKING
—OUR—
PERSONALITY

CHAPTER SIX

Personality Assessment: Describing and Testing Personality

Did you see that personality in the corner of the room? Were you able to touch it?

Ridiculous questions. You can't see personality and you can't touch it. Yet, psychologists have had to find a way to talk about personality, describe it, and measure it. We need to know how one person's personality is different from another person's. We need to be able to describe what makes each of us special. That's where tests of personality come in.

THE FIRST "TESTS" OF PERSONALITY

The idea for testing what we now call personality is not new.[1] Throughout history, people have been trying to find ways to predict how others might behave in different circumstances. For example, they wanted to know whether a particular person would make a good church member. Would a person be a good worker or a good soldier? Could someone be trusted to keep the queen's jewels safe?

One of the earliest methods for assessing such questions was astrology. Based on the positions of the stars when a person was born, astrologers made predictions about how he or she might behave in the future. This is obviously an indirect way to guess what kind of person someone was!

Another method, coming after astrology, was something called physiognomy (fis-ee-ogno-mee). This was a system developed by the ancient Greeks. The physical features of people's heads, the expressions on their faces, the shape of their bodies, and the way they walked, among other things, were measured. These things were believed to provide clues about an individual's personality.

MODERN METHODS OF TESTING PERSONALITY

Today, most people don't think that the stars in the sky or the way a person looks says much about how they might behave most of the time. Instead, psychologists have created *personality tests.*

Personality tests have been "tried out" on many people before they're officially used. Because many people have taken the test, we know how most people answer the questions. We can then compare one person's answers with the answers of larger groups of people and see how they are the same and how they are different. If someone's answer is very different from the answer that hundreds of other people might have given, we can assume that the answer is telling us a little bit about how he or she is different and special. We could then look at the special answers and try to say something about what it might mean about personality.

Personality tests try to measure the traits and behaviors that are unique to a person in many different ways. Some of these tests are similar to surveys that you may have answered about such things as your favorite foods or favorite music. Some tests ask people to use their imaginations and talk about what they "see" in certain designs and pictures. Other methods rely on a therapist who asks a person questions about his or her life and beliefs. Finally, some researchers actually observe people doing their ordinary daily activities. We'll discuss each of these types next.

SELF-REPORT TESTS

People taking a *self-report test* are asked to report on their own feelings and personal characteristics or traits. Usually, people are given a series of statements. They are asked to answer each one by checking off whether it is true or false or by saying how much they agree or disagree with the statement. Obviously, the test can't ask about everything a person has ever done, thought, or said. But the answers they give provide psychologists with an idea about some of their important personality traits by comparing them with the answers of many others.

Probably the most famous self-report test is the *MMPI*.[2] (Its full name is "Minnesota Multiphasic Personality Inventory"). The test has statements covering many different aspects of personality. People taking the test are asked to check whether each statement is true or false about themselves. (Or they can check a box labeled "cannot say" if they're not sure.)

The MMPI was originally developed to help mental health workers tell whether or not a person taking the test was similar to certain types of mental patients. As we described above, the person's answers would be compared with groups of mental patients. If the answers of the person taking the test were very similar to the answers of groups of patients with mental illness, then it might be likely that the person taking the test also has that illness. Of course, a mental health worker would never rely only on this test to make that diagnosis. Other tests, as well as information that the therapist obtained from the patient and people who know the patient, would have to agree.

Aside from its help in finding out if a person might have a mental illness, the MMPI has been used as a more general test of personality because it also gives us information about a lot of different feelings and behaviors. Many thousands of people have taken the test and we know how they have responded to its items. The test has been used to predict if a police officer will use a weapon, if a particular person would make a good athlete, and if someone will succeed in college.[3]

Some of the items included in the test are just statements about a person's mood ("I am happy most of the time"). Some are about behaviors and preferences ("I go to a party every week," "I forgive people easily," "I sometimes enjoy breaking the law," "I would like to be a soldier"). Others are about things that most people don't experience ("Voices speak to me in the night," "Someone is pouring dirty thoughts into my head"). Remember, it is the pattern of answers that someone gives compared with the answers of other groups of people that tells us about the test taker's personality.

When the MMPI is used properly, the results are useful. However, it is sometimes used incorrectly. For instance, if it were the only test given to a person, and a judgment was made about a person's mental illness just on the basis of his or her score on this test, it would not be used properly. In the same way, if it were used for a purpose that it was not intended—such as to see whether a person would make a good carpenter—it also might not be helpful. Therefore, it is crucial when using a test to be sure it is being used correctly.

Another type of self-report test measures a person's interests in a variety of different activities. Such a test can be used to tell us something about what kind of job they might be good at. One example of this kind of test is the *Strong Vocational Interest Blank* (SVIB). This test contains hundreds of items asking about a wide number of activities and interests. A person taking the SVIB is asked to say whether they like, dislike, or have no feeling about such things as different occupations, school subjects, activities, and hobbies.[4] Examples might include fixing a radio, talking to a group of people at a lecture, or working to make money for charity. The test results provide a pattern of a person's likes and dislikes. Because we already know the pattern of likes and dislikes of people who are in different occupations, we can compare the two.

For instance, large numbers of dentists, social workers, sales people, bank tellers, and so forth have been tested, and we know what pattern of answers they give. If the pattern of likes, dislikes, and special interests of a person taking the test is very similar, for example, to the pattern of dentists, then we could expect that the individual is likely to be satisfied doing what dentists do. This is useful information for someone trying to decide what to study in school or what skills to practice.

Interest tests provide a list of possible occupations that the person tested would be likely to find appealing. They compare the interests of the test taker with that of people already successful in many different occupations. The theory is that if you like the same kind of things as do people in a certain occupation, you are likely to be successful in that occupation.

However, interest tests don't tell what people's abilities are. Even though someone might find the activities of a job interesting, that's no guarantee that they will have the skills to be good at it.

PROJECTIVE PERSONALITY TESTS

People who accept Freud's psychoanalytic theory (which we discussed in Chapter 2) believe that a person's behavior is sometimes caused by things they cannot see, know, or talk about directly because they are hidden in the unconscious. If they think this and want to learn about someone's personality, they would need to find a way to test what was going on in the unconscious part of personality.

In order to look into the unconscious, psychologists have created *projective tests.* In projective tests, the person being tested is shown a test item (such as a drawing) that is ambiguous (am-big-you-us), or without clear meaning. For example, an ambiguous drawing could look equally like a father having a nice conversation with his son or a father scolding his son. Because the drawing has no clear meaning, people taking the test make up their own meaning.

Psychoanalysts believe that what the person sees in the drawing tells us something about how the person interprets things in the world. What the person sees comes from that person's unconscious mind. The unconscious mind "projects" a person's inner thoughts onto what they say they see in the drawing—just as a movie projector projects the images of a movie onto a blank screen.

If you were to take one of these tests, chances are you would take the *Rorschach* (roar-shock) *test.*[5] When you take this test, you are shown ten cards, one at a time. Each card has a design on it that looks a lot like an inkblot. (If you've ever spilled some paint or ink on a piece of paper, folded the paper over to "blot" up the spill, and then opened it up, you would know what an inkblot might look like.) The inkblot designs don't have any meaning in themselves.

You would be asked by the examiner what the design might mean. The examiner would write down your answer and ask you questions about what you saw, where on the card you saw it, and how many different things you could see in each design. The examiner might also tell you what other people usually see in the designs and ask if you also saw them.

Once you've given your responses, the examiner compares your answers with the answers of many other types of people by using an instruction manual that tells how to interpret your answers. For example, it is believed that if you see a bear in one of the designs, you may have a lot of control over how you express your feelings. The examiner also looks for different "themes" in your answers. If you repeatedly see animals getting ripped apart and beaten, one interpretation might be that you are very angry. A lot of water in your answers might mean you have concerns about alcoholism; a lot of eyes might mean that you are too suspicious.

Another common projective test of personality is the *Thematic Apperception Test* (TAT). In this test, a person is shown a series of up to thirty pictures, one at a time. The pictures resemble old-time movie scenes; they are in black, white, and shades of gray. Most of the pictures have at least one person in them doing something. But, because this is a projective test, it is not really clear exactly what's going on.

It's up to the person taking the test to tell a story about what came before the scene in the picture, what's happening in the picture, who in the picture is thinking and feeling what, and how it will end up. The person tells a story about each picture to the examiner who writes down the story and its details. The examiner might also ask questions after each story to get more information.

Let's use an example to show how this test might say something about someone's personality. Suppose that one of the pictures shows a man in a suit coat and tie coming into a house or apartment through a door. The person taking the test would be asked to tell a complete story about this picture. He or she might tell a story about a father coming home after a day at work. (In fact, this type of picture is expected to get people to tell stories about their fathers.)

In telling the story, the person taking the test might talk about how the man was angry and mean and didn't care about his family, would ignore his wife and children, and then go to sleep. The story might end by saying that his kids would grow up to hate him and never get along with anyone older.

If the person's other stories contained fathers (or older men who controlled their employees) who were uncaring and ignored the wishes of their children, this might show that the person had trouble expressing anger when someone was angry with him or her. This might be particularly true in work or family situations.

As tests of personality, projective tests have one special advantage and one special disadvantage.[6] Their biggest advantage is that the people taking the test can say whatever they want in response to each item. They don't have to say whether something is just true or false or whether they like it or not. Their personality is therefore felt to be "revealed" most easily by this type of test.

On the other hand, the greatest disadvantage is the freedom that people have to say whatever they want. Also their answers have to be interpreted so freely that it's almost entirely up to the person scoring the test to say what it means. If that person is wrong, careless, biased, or if the interpreter's unconscious mind makes him or her interpret the test poorly, the results of the test don't mean much.

BEHAVIORAL ASSESSMENT

A final important way of learning about personality comes from behavioral theories about personality. Psychologists who believe that learning theory is the most important way to understand personality don't believe in indirect methods of finding out about people. They don't accept the idea of the unconscious. They don't believe that how someone tells a story or what they see in a design says much about what is important about them as a person. They also think that there is no better way to find out about a person than by directly watching them and talking with them.

Behavioral assessment is a system for doing just that.[7] It can be done right in a person's home, school, workplace, or the psychologist's office. Behavioral assessment tries to record specific activities or events, such as the number of times someone behaves a certain way, the length of time each behavior takes, and so forth.

For instance, if you were interested in knowing how aggressive a child was, you could count the number of times the child yelled at or hit someone during a class at school. Similarly, if you wanted to know how important being cooperative was to someone, you could count the number of times the person completed a project involving cooperation with others. In either case, you would be counting something you saw and some-thing the person actually did.

This system is particularly good at figuring out what types of behavior lead to other behaviors you might be interested in. Suppose you wanted to know what makes it more likely that a two year old would have a temper tantrum. You could observe what came before and after a tantrum, and you might also then learn what things calmed the child down and led to fewer tantrums. You could use this information to change the child's behavior.

Some behavioral psychologists have decided that it is not enough to just watch someone behave and record it. It is also important to pay attention to things we cannot see, such as how or what a person thinks. If a boy is fighting with a girl at school, a behavioral psychologist might want to talk to him and ask what he was thinking before he fought with the girl. He might want to help the boy think something different the next time this happened. These behavioral psychologists are called *cognitive behaviorists.* The word cogni-tive refers to thinking and this is an approach to behavioral assessment that is becoming more popular.

WHICH METHOD OF PERSONALITY TESTING IS BEST?

As you can see, psychologists have developed dif-ferent methods for assessing personality. The particular methods a psychologist might use to test any one individual depend on several things.

First is the purpose for which the test is being taken. If someone wants help in figuring out what occupation he or she might be most interested in, an interest test would be used. If there is a need to find out whether someone has a psychological disorder, a combination of self-report tests and projective tests would be used. If advice about ways to change the behavior of children in a class is needed, behavioral assessment might be most appropriate.

In addition to the purpose for which the test is being given, the methods selected also depend on what the psychologist believes about how best to explain personality. Obviously, a behaviorist will not use projective tests, because behaviorists believe there are more direct and better ways to understand behavior. A psychoanalyst would be much more interested in knowing about what unconscious forces were causing behavior. Projective tests would be used in that case.

One thing is clear. There is no one best method. All methods are useful depending on what we want to know and what we believe about how best to explain personality.

CHAPTER SEVEN

Personality and Identity

So far, we've defined personality, described several ideas about how personality develops, and tried to specify the key parts of personality. We've also talked about different types of personality problems and how psychologists describe and test for many different aspects of personality. What we have not yet discussed is how your sense of who you are develops.

Psychologists have a term for your sense of yourself, or your description to yourself of who you are. That term is *identity*. When we talk about your identity, we are talking about characteristics of who you are, including

1. What kind of person you are.
2. The kinds of skills you have.
3. The jobs you might want to have.

4. The way you see yourself fitting into the rest of the world.
5. The contributions you see yourself making to other people and your community.
6. The roles you play in your family and with your friends.

In a way, you might think of your identity as the "inside view" of your personality. Your identity is composed of the things that are important to you and give meaning to your life.

But identity also refers to something else. It is a stage you must reach. You are not born with an identity. In fact, psychologists say that you have not yet formed an identity even in childhood.

Identity is a special stage of development that has to be reached in the teenage or early adult years. Most people develop an identity at this time. Some people never really get there. We'll talk about why later in the chapter.

DEVELOPING AN IDENTITY

In the chapter on psychoanalytic theory (Chapter 2), we discussed Freud's theory about how personality develops. He described how a child develops a personality by going through a series of stages. At each stage, the child's ego learns to cope with the demands for pleasure from his or her id as well as the demands to try to be perfect coming from the superego. There is a tension between these two forces with which the ego has to cope.

You might think of it as a conflict between opposing forces, in this case the three parts to personality called id, ego, and superego. However, all these forces come from inside the child. Remember that the id, ego, and superego are said to be inside the mind of the developing child. You might think of the way personality develops, according to Freud, this way. The forces inside the child "mold" his or her personality pretty much the way a sculptor molds clay. The way these forces end up molding the child creates her or his personality. And, as you already know, Freud believed that this molding was done by the time the child got to the teenage years.

Another psychoanalyst created an additional theory of development. This theory is different from Freud's ideas, which emphasize the conflict between the opposing forces inside the mind of the developing person.

Instead, this theory stresses the way in which the person learns to cope with the requirements of the world outside oneself. It is a theory of how the mind, or the developing personality, is shaped or molded by the world in which the child lives.

The kind of theory we're talking about is called a *psychosocial* (sy-ko-so-shull) *theory* of development. A psychosocial theory of development emphasizes the basic fact that we all live in a social world. As a part of growing up, children have to learn to get along with their parents, friends, community, and society in general.

The person who created this psychosocial theory was Erik Erikson. As we've indicated above, Erikson's theory shows how a number of stages of development lead to the opportunity for people to develop what we call an identity—a special sense of who they are and where they fit in the world. Erikson also believed that people continue to develop their personalities all through their lives.

Erikson's psychosocial theory is like Freud's in at least one way: the belief that personality develops in stages. But Erikson emphasized the way that the individual behaves as he or she has to interact with other people. The stages have to be worked on one at a time, just as in some math problems where there are several steps and you need the answer to one step before you can go on to the next. In addition, success in solving the issues posed at one stage affect success at the next stage. As with math problems, if you get the wrong answer on the first step, you would not be able to find the right answer to the second one either.

Each stage has a name that is based on the concerns that are most important to people during the stage. The issues are similar to challenges that the person has to meet,[1] just as a runner might have to get over certain hurdles at a track meet. The issue can be worked out well, in which case personality is made stronger, or the issue might not be worked out so well, in which case personality might be weakened.

Erikson first described his theory in a book called *Childhood and Society*.[2] We will first briefly describe all the stages and then focus on the stage in which Erikson spoke most about the development of identity. (The stages are summarized in Table 2.)

The first stage is called "trust versus mistrust" and covers the age of infancy. If infants can rely on their parents or caretakers to meet their needs (food, holding, dry diapers, etc.), they develop a basic trust for the world. If not, they may fear that others will not take care of them.

The next stage, "autonomy versus shame and doubt," covers the years of early childhood. In this stage, if caretakers trust and encourage their children to explore their own environment, children will learn that they can rely on themselves. If not, children will have trouble with being on their own.

The stage of "initiative versus guilt" occurs in the preschool years. Children learn to start activities independently if their parents encourage them. If not, children may feel that they have done something wrong or that it is too risky to try new things.

By the time children enter school, and throughout the elementary school years, children are working on the stage of "industry versus inferiority." Children build necessary skills in school and recreational activities, as well as learn how to have

TABLE 2. A Summary of Erikson's Stages

Stage	Approximate Age	Positive Outcomes	Negative Outcomes
Trust vs. mistrust	Birth–1½ years	Feelings of trust from environmental support	Fear and concern regarding others
Autonomy vs. shame and doubt	1½–3 years	Self-sufficiency if exploration is encouraged	Doubts about self, lack of independence
Initiative vs. guilt	3–6 years	Discovery of ways to initiate actions	Guilt from actions and thoughts
Industry vs. inferiority	6–12 years	Development of sense of competence	Feelings of inferiority, no sense of mastery
Identity vs. role confusion	Adolescence	Awareness of uniqueness of self, knowledge of role to be followed	Inability to identify appropriate roles in life
Intimacy vs. isolation	Early adulthood	Development of loving, sexual relationships and close friendships	Fear of relationships with others
Generativity vs. stagnation	Middle adulthood	Sense of contribution to continuity of life	Trivialization of one's activities
Ego-integrity vs. despair	Late adulthood	Sense of unity in life's accomplishments	Regret over lost opportunities of life

friendships and relationships with family. If they don't do this well, children have a sense of failure and inferiority.

The next stage is called "identity versus role confusion." Here, teenagers establish a strong sense of themselves and feel secure about the things that are important in life. Or, they end up confused, unsure of who they are, and uncertain how to dedicate their life.

Following this stage, people are in the young adult years. This part of development is called "intimacy versus isolation." Success in this stage means finding the ability to develop close relationships and commitments to others. If this stage is not passed through successfully, people become anxious and unsuccessful in relationships.

In middle adulthood, people are considering the issues of "generativity versus stagnation." If the stage works out well, people have a sense of really being able to make a contribution to their community, family, and friends. They have a general sense that they are a success at what is important to them. If not, they lack a sense of being able to be respected for what they are doing.

The final stage of personality development is called "integrity versus despair" and covers the senior-citizen years until death. Here, if all goes well, people feel that their entire lives have made a difference to themselves and the world. If it does not work out well, people feel that life has been relatively meaningless. They have a lot of regrets about what they might have been able to do with their lives.

By living through these stages and working out the challenges at each stage, Erikson felt that the personality was continually developing. Even if a certain stage did not work out in the best possible way, people could still work on that challenge in later life (although it would "slow them down" in working on later challenges).

IDENTITY VERSUS ROLE CONFUSION

Let's return for a moment and consider the stage that is probably most important in Erikson's theory: identity versus role confusion. This stage is especially critical to teenagers. It is in this stage that people first must find a way to put together all their skills, abilities, preferences, and values, to end up with a consistent and important sense of who they are.

If things work out well, it is in this stage that individuals say to themselves and to the world, "This is who I am, and this is how I'm special and unique." This process permits them to form a strong identity that will guide their personality development for the rest of their lives. If a person is unable to do this well, he or she may end up confused about what to do in life, how to be a friend to someone, and too ready to "drop out" of life (in other words, role confusion).

How does this happen? You have to remember that the teenage years are a time of great personal, social, and physical changes. All these changes force adolescents to adjust. As part of this adjustment, they have to seriously think about their appearance, their friendships, and how they relate to their family, teachers, and other adults. They also have to find a way to work out who they are sexually. Many adolescents also begin to understand and be concerned about important issues in the world such as justice, hunger, war and peace, philosophy, and politics. Finally, toward the end of the teenage years, most also have to think about jobs or careers and independence from their families.

Most often, all these challenges occur a few at a time and are manageable, though even the most self-confident teenager can, at times, get overwhelmed and upset by all this. Sometimes, however, the force of having to work out so many important things at a time when everything seems to be changing leads to some sense of distress. Whether they are managed easily or with distress, this is the time of the adolescent *identity crisis.*

Don't be confused by the word "crisis." This does not mean that people fall apart or are in great trouble. But to develop a strong sense of identity at this stage, adolescents must seriously consider their lives, their choices for the future, and the aspects of their personality that they value and cherish. The way that "crisis" is used here means it is a time of serious consideration of how people want to be involved with family, friends, and the world.

Erikson felt that the most important part of this stage involved the adolescents' relationships with family, peers, and other adults who are important to them.[3] As teenagers "try out" new roles, ways of behaving, different ways of talking, and even new styles of dressing, they are also looking at the ways others respond to them. If someone really matters to them, they will find a way to make that person's reaction part of their identity.

Because all this happens at a time in life when changes take place so fast, you might question where adolescents get the time for all this serious consideration of their lives. Erikson talked about something called a "psychosocial moratorium," which takes place during this stage of development.

The word moratorium (more-uh-tor-ee-yum) means a time of life when definite decisions don't have to be made. It's like a timeout in sports or a ceasefire in a battle. Strategies or ideas can be tried out before being put into action. Consequently, psychological moritorium means that during the teenage years, it is expected that no lifelong commitment to a way of life has to be decided.

In a way, the secondary school years (and even early college years, if a person goes to college), provide a time when new roles and identities can be "tried out." Careers or jobs can be considered and examined, and experience in holding a job can be gained. Family roles may be

101

challenged and changed. Relationships provide a place to argue and learn about important things in the world. Sexuality gets considered, and for some, is explored. These years before adulthood are a place and time to try out parts of your identity before having to go your own way and settle into a job and perhaps a family.

HOW THE IDENTITY-VERSUS-ROLE-CONFU-SION STAGE IS RESOLVED As you remember, the identity-versus-role-confusion stage can be worked out (or "resolved") well, or it might not get worked out to the person's best advantage. If it is resolved well, people develop an understanding of who they are, and they will feel that they have achieved something important. People will have a strong sense of what's important to them and "where they are going" in their lives. In short, they will have gone through a time of "crisis" and they will have made a strong "commitment" to important areas of their life.

But what if this stage is not worked out well? According to Erikson, problems in resolving the identity-versus-role-confusion stage lead to a weak identity. There are several different outcomes that are possible.[4]

For instance, some people who don't consider their options and don't question themselves about important things don't go through an identity crisis. Instead, they just seem to settle on the career that their parents (or someone else important to them) always expected them to choose. It's as if they were placed on a track when they were young and they just followed that track because it was there. Even so, these people do end up forming an identity.

They may, however, miss out on reaching their full potential in life because they have not really considered all their options. Their identity might not be as complete as it might be because the normal process for forming an identity (going through a period of "crisis") has been interrupted. Resolving the identity-versus-role-confusion stage in this way ends up in what is called identity foreclosure.

Other people seem neither to have an identity crisis nor to come out of adolescence with a strong sense of commitment to jobs, family, and values. When the stage of identity versus role confusion is ended without a sense of commitment and without having gone through an identity crisis, the result is a condition called identity diffusion.

People who fall in this category may remain confused for some time, wandering through jobs and life almost without any plans. Since they have no firm ideas about how they should be, they are not likely to form close relationships or to make progress toward a career. Or, they may not care much about anything and drift through life.

In sum, this stage can be resolved by going through an identity crisis and coming out of the psychosocial moratorium time with a strong set of commitments to work, family and friends, and values. If this happens, people come through this time in a good position to deal with the next stage of life.

People who have made commitments in this stage, and who have done it by going through a time of crisis, are what is called identity achievers.[5] Not only do they feel that they have accomplished something important in learning about themselves and the world, but they are also able to deal with change and stress and to adjust to life's demands fairly well.

CHAPTER EIGHT

Can Personality Be Changed?

Think back to how personality was described at the beginning of this book. We said that personality was made up of the characteristics that make us distinctive from others and are consistent over time.

This definition of personality might lead us to believe that we couldn't do very much to change our personalities. After all, if personality is "consistent over time," we wouldn't expect that it could be changed very much once it is formed.

However, this is not the case. We are not stuck with every aspect of our personality for our entire lives. Of course, some parts of personality are not easily changed. Some characteristics are so central to the kind of people that we are that they are resistant to alteration.

But some aspects of personality can be

changed. We'll consider two ways of changing parts of personality. One comes from altering the way we think about the world. The other comes from directly changing our behavior.

CHANGING YOUR THINKING

Your teacher hands back the science test you took last week. You look at the grade with a sinking feeling: it's an "F." You feel miserable, and you find yourself saying things to yourself like this:

> *"I'm a total failure in life."*
> *"I'll never succeed in school."*
> *"I'm the stupidest person in the world."*

Wrong! This kind of thinking doesn't make any sense. Doing poorly on one test doesn't mean your life is doomed to failure. It just means that you did badly on one test.

Unfortunately, many of us think these kinds of thoughts. If someone is mean to us, we may say to ourselves, "People are never nice to me." If we can't find something we lost, we may think, "I lose everything."

This kind of thinking is called catastrophic thinking.[1] In *catastrophic thinking,* we turn a minor matter into a life-or-death one. Instead of looking at things that happen to us as something that we can change, we think about them as things that can never be altered.

Catastrophic thinking is not only inaccurate,

but thinking such thoughts can actually *make* it more likely that the events we fear will occur in the future. The reason is that this kind of thinking can become a self-fulfilling prophecy.[2] A *self-fulfilling prophecy* is a prediction that comes true because we act in ways that make the prediction become a reality. If we hadn't made the prediction, it might not have come true. But after we've made a prediction, we may act in ways that makes sure it happens.

As an example of a self-fulfilling prophecy, suppose you say to yourself that you're sure that you're going to do badly in school. Because you think you're going to do badly, you may spend so much time worrying that you don't try very hard or study much. Because of all this worrying, then, you end up not doing well.

Of course, it could have been different. If you had tried harder and studied more, you would have actually done better. Therefore, it is your inaccurate thinking that made you fail. You have been the victim of a self-fulfilling prophecy.

Psychologists feel that many of us are guilty of thinking in ways that make us fail. We have unrealistic thoughts that prevent us from making the situation better.

There is a solution, though. You can stop this kind of thinking. You can stop telling yourself inaccurate and self-defeating thoughts. Instead, when you have such a thought, you can come up with a more reasonable response, one that allows you to deal with the situation.

For example, suppose you're taking a test, and you feel that you don't know the material. Instead of going into a panic, you can deal with the catastrophic thoughts you have. If you find yourself thinking, "This test is so hard I'm sure to flunk," think instead, "There may be parts that are hard, but some questions are easier and I can do well on them." If you think, "My mind is a blank; I don't remember a thing," say to yourself, "I've studied this material and knew it earlier today, so I'm sure to remember some of it later."

The goal is to think of ways to deal with the catastrophic thoughts. Instead of letting thoughts that are not rational come true, try to think in a more logical way. The more often you try this, the less frequently you'll think of catastrophic thoughts.

Can you change your personality by modifying the way you think? In some cases, yes. By thinking more logically, you will be less likely to be the victim of self-fulfilling prophecies. Because you view the world more accurately, you may be able to act in more reasonable ways.

Of course, not every part of personality can be changed by thinking in a more rational way. But some important aspects can be modified.

CHANGING YOUR BEHAVIOR

You may remember from Chapter 3 that some psychologists interested in personality focus not on how we think but on how we behave. To them, if we want to bring about a change in people's personalities, the best way is to change their behavior directly.

The process of changing behavior is called self-management. In *self-management*,[3] a person selects a behavior that he or she wants to change and then develops a plan to change it. For instance, self-management can be used to become a neater person, to work harder, or even to lose weight. It is useful for many kinds of problem behaviors that people might want to change, and it can help people modify important aspects of their personalities.

Self-management can be done in many ways. However, the same basic procedure can be used in most cases: New, desired behaviors are rewarded. At the same time, the environment is changed to make it less likely that old, unwanted behaviors will reoccur.

Consider this example of self-management: Suppose you're shy and you feel that people sometimes walk all over you. You want to become more assertive, raising your self-confidence. You decide to try self-management.

The first thing you need to do is to find out the conditions under which you need to be assertive. For instance, it might be that whenever someone asks you for a favor, you can't say "No." This makes you feel bad, because you sense that others take advantage of you.

To remedy your lack of assertiveness, you would try to set up a number of goals and rules about being assertive. For instance, you might decide on the rule that you'll always refuse people's requests at first, telling them that you'll "think about it." You'll then have more time to decide whether you really want to do them the favor.

In order to be successful in carrying out the "rule," you'll need practice. You might pretend that someone has asked you for a favor, and practice saying (out loud) that you'll think about it. Or you might ask a good friend to practice with you. Have the friend pretend to ask you for a favor, and then practice saying that you'll think about it. The important thing is to get as much practice as you can. Then, when someone really asks for a favor, you'll be ready.

It is also important to build in a system to reward yourself. Whenever you are able to refuse a request for a favor, you might treat yourself to an ice cream cone or candy bar. And if you can't refuse, you might force yourself to give a dollar to someone you don't like. In this way, you increase your chances of becoming more assertive.

Self-management can't be used to modify every aspect of people's personalities. Some parts of personality are so deeply established that self-management won't work. However, some important changes are possible.

PERSONALITY CHANGE THROUGH THERAPY

We've seen two examples of ways that people can try to change personality. One is through modifying how people think about the world, and the other is by directly changing people's behavior. These procedures are often useful for altering specific feelings and behaviors that people are unhappy about. They can also help people to get the most out of their abilities and experiences.

If personality change is not too involved, it may be possible for people to use such methods on their own. But in many cases, people are unable to bring about personality change by themselves.

For example, sometimes people's unhappiness with their personality is so deep that they can't find ways to produce change by themselves. In other cases, the personality trait that people may wish to change is so fundamental to their personality that they are unable to bring about change alone.

In such cases, *psychological therapy* may be called for. Psychological therapy consists of meeting with a professional in order to remedy concerns and difficulties about life.

There are many kinds of therapy. In fact, some estimates suggest that there are over 250 different kinds. However, there is a common thread among them: the goal is to produce psychological change through discussions and interactions between a person and a therapist. The therapist acts as an unbiased sounding board, encouraging people to see their strengths and weaknesses. The therapist helps them to choose a good route to bringing about improvements in their lives.

Of course, not every aspect of personality can be changed through therapy. In fact, there is argument among experts on personality about just how much people can change their basic characteristics.

There is also disagreement on which methods of personality change are best. It seems to be true, though, that all the methods work some of the time. It depends a lot on which methods make sense to the person wanting to change. After all, she or he will be the one doing the work. The key is for people to trust the person who is trying to help them change. They need to find a method that is a "good fit" between their therapist and their personality.

Some theories suggest that changing personality characteristics takes a long time and a lot of work. For example, Freud's psychoanalytic theory (discussed in Chapter 2) says that personality is basically formed early in life. Furthermore, in psychoanalytic theory much of adult behavior is thought to ruled by unconscious forces.

Because of these views, psychoanalytic explanations of personality say that personality change is a lengthy and time-consuming process. It involves developing a relationship with a therapist over time. This relationship helps people to experience and understand basic problems in their lives. Once they can experience their problems and understand them with their therapist, they don't have to go on avoiding them by keeping them in their unconscious.

Other theories say personality change can occur much more quickly during therapy. For example, people in therapy can be taught to change their thinking patterns or modify their behavior in the ways that we discussed earlier in the chapter. Because these explanations do not see personality as produced by out-of-reach, unconscious forces, personality change can occur much more rapidly.

There is also no clear answer to the question of how *much* can personality be changed. Plainly, some parts of personality can be changed if people want to devote the effort to change things about themselves. But if personality consists of the characteristics that make people consistent, then too much change probably is not possible, or even desirable.

For instance, if the behavior of people around us was never consistent, we would be unable to predict how they would behave. This would make life extremely complex and puzzling. In the same way, if *we* had no unique and consistent ways of behaving, every situation would present us with a new challenge. We would always be at the mercy of whatever circumstances we found ourselves in, because we would have no consistent way of behaving.

In sum, personality provides a foundation for our behavior, guiding our behavior and that of others. Although we may be able to change some aspects of personality, we also have to learn to accept our basic characteristics. Learning about— and accepting—who we are is crucial to our well-being.

SOURCE NOTES

CHAPTER 1

1. E. J. Phares, *Introduction to Personality* (3rd ed.), (New York: Harper Collins, 1991).

CHAPTER 2

1. B. E. Moore, and B. D. Fine, *Psychoanalytic Terms and Concepts* (New Haven, Conn.: Yale University Press, 1990).
2. S. Freud, *The Basic Writings of Sigmund Freud* (New York: Modern Library, 1938).
3. D. Westen, "Psychoanalytic Approaches to Personality." In L.A. Pervin (Ed.), *Handbook of Personality* (New York: Guilford, 1990).

CHAPTER 3

1. A. H. Maslow, *Motivation and Personality* (3rd ed.), (New York: Harper & Row, 1987).
2. B. F. Skinner, *Beyond Freedom and Dignity.* (New York: Knopf, 1971).
3. A. Bandura, *Social Foundations of Thought and Action: A Social Cognitive Theory* (Englewood Cliffs, NJ: Prentice-Hall, 1986).

CHAPTER 4

1. G. Allport, *Pattern and Growth in Personality* (New York: Holt, Rinehart & Winston, 1961). G. W. Allport, "Traits revisited." *American Psychologist,* 1961, no. 21: 1–10.
2. R. B. Cattell, *The Scientific Analysis of Personality.* (Baltimore: Penguin, 1967).
3. H. J. Eysenck, and M. W. Eysenck, *Personality and Individual Differences: A Natural Science Approach.* (New York: Plenum, 1985).
4. D. C. Funder and C.R. Colvin, "Explorations in behavioral consistency: Properties of persons, situations, and behaviors." *Journal of Personality and Social Psychology,* 1991, no. 60: 773–94.

CHAPTER 5

1. R. Bootzin and J.R. Acocella, *Abnormal Psychology: Current Perspectives* (5th ed.) (New York: Random House, 1988).
2. American Psychiatric Association, *Diagnostic*

and Statistical Manual of Mental Disorders (3rd ed., revised) (Washington, D.C.: American Psychiatric Association Press, 1987).

CHAPTER 6

1. C. Gorney, "The Many Faces of S.: A Question of Rape," *Washington Post,* 6 November 1990, 113, C1.
2. American Psychiatric Association, *Diagnostic and Statistical Manual of Mental Disorders* (3rd ed., revised) (Washington, D.C.: American Psychiatric Association Press, 1987).
3. B. Braun, "New Focus on Multiple Personality," (D. Goleman interview), New York Times, 21 May 1985, C1.
4. American Psychiatric Association, *Diagnostic and Statistical Manual of Mental Disorders* (3rd ed., revised), (Washington, D.C.: American Psychiatric Association Press, 1987).
5. and 6. R. Bootzin, and J. R. Acocella, *Abnormal Psychology: Current Perspectives* (5th ed.) (New York: Random House, 1988).
7. C.H. Thigpen and H. Cleckley. *The Three Faces of Eve.* (New York: McGraw-Hill, 1957).
8. American Psychiatric Association, *Diagnostic and Statistical Manual of Mental Disorders* (3rd ed., revised), (Washington, D.C.: American Psychiatric Association Press, 1987).
9. American Psychiatric Association, *Diagnostic and Statistical Manual of Mental Disorders*

(3rd ed., revised), (Washington, D.C.: American Psychiatric Association Press, 1987).

10. CBS News, *Sixty Minutes: "The Trials of Juanita,"* 29 September 1991.

11. Associated Press Report, 12 March 1991.

CHAPTER 7

1. and 4. A. Anastasi, *Psychological Testing* (3rd ed.), (London, England: MacMillan, 1966).

2. S.R. Hathaway, and J.C. McKinley, *MMPI-2: Minnesota Multiphasic Personality Inventory-2* (Minneapolis: University of Minnesota Press, 1989).

3. C. Holden, "Researchers Grapple with Problems of Updating Classic Psychological Test," *Science,* 19 September 1986, no. 233: 1249–51.

5. H. Rorschach, *Psychodiagnosis: A Diagnostic Test Based on Perception* (New York: Grune & Stratton, 1924).

6. R. Bootzin, and J.R. Acocella, *Abnormal Psychology: Current Perspectives* (5th ed.) (New York: Random House, 1988).

7. B. Sulzer-Azaroff, and R. Mayer, *Behavior Analysis for Lasting Change.* (Fort Worth: Holt, Rinehart, & Winston, 1991).

CHAPTER 8

1. and 4. L. Steinberg, *Adolescence* (2nd ed.) (New York: Alfred A. Knopf, 1989).

2. E.H. Erikson, *Childhood and Society.* (New York: Norton, 1950).
3. J.E. Marcia, "Development and Validation of Ego Identity Status," *Journal of Personality and Social Psychology,* 1966, *3,* 551–58.

CHAPTER 9

1. A. Ellis, and R. Grieger, *Handbook of Rational Emotive Therapy* (New York: Springer Verlag, 1977).
2. W.P. Archibald, "Alternative Explanations for the Self-Fulfilling Prophecy." *Psychological Bulletin,* 1974, *821,* 74–84.
3. B. Sulzer-Azaroff, and R. Mayer, *Behavior Analysis for Lasting Change* (Fort Worth: Holt, Rinehart, & Winston, 1991).

FOR FURTHER READING

Anastasi, A. *Psychological Testing* (3rd ed.). London, England: MacMillan, 1966.

Elkind, D. *All Grown Up and No Place to Go: Teenagers in Crisis.* Reading, Mass.: Addison-Wesley, 1984.

Erikson, E.H. *Identity: Youth and Crisis.* New York: Norton, 1968.

Freud, S. *New Introductory Lectures on Psychoanalysis.* London: Hogarth Press, 1962.

Hall, C.S., & Lindzey, G. *Theories of Personality* (3rd ed.) New York: Wiley, 1978.

Kanfer, F.H., & Goldstein, A.P. (Eds.) *Helping People Change* (3rd ed.) New York: Pergamon Press, 1985.

Peterson, C. *Personality.* San Diego: Harcourt Brace Jovanovich, 1988.

Sweetland, R.C., & Keyser, D.J. *Tests: A Comprehensive Reference for Assessments in Psychology, Education, Business* (2nd ed.) Kansas City, Mo.: Test Corporation of America, 1988.

Thigpen, C.H., & Cleckley, H. *The Three Faces of Eve.* New York: McGraw-Hill, 1957.

INDEX

ABOUT THE AUTHORS

Robert S. Feldman, Ph.D., Professor of Psychology at the University of Massachusetts in Amherst, Massachusetts, is the author of *Understanding Psychology,* a bestselling college textbook. He has also written *Understanding Stress* for the Franklin Watts Venture Book series.

Joel A. Feinman, Ph.D., a clinical psychologist, is Director of Mental Health Services for the Northeast Permanente Medical Group of Massachusetts.